Vol 7

MAZE

FOR KIDS

Ages 4-6

MAZE BOOK

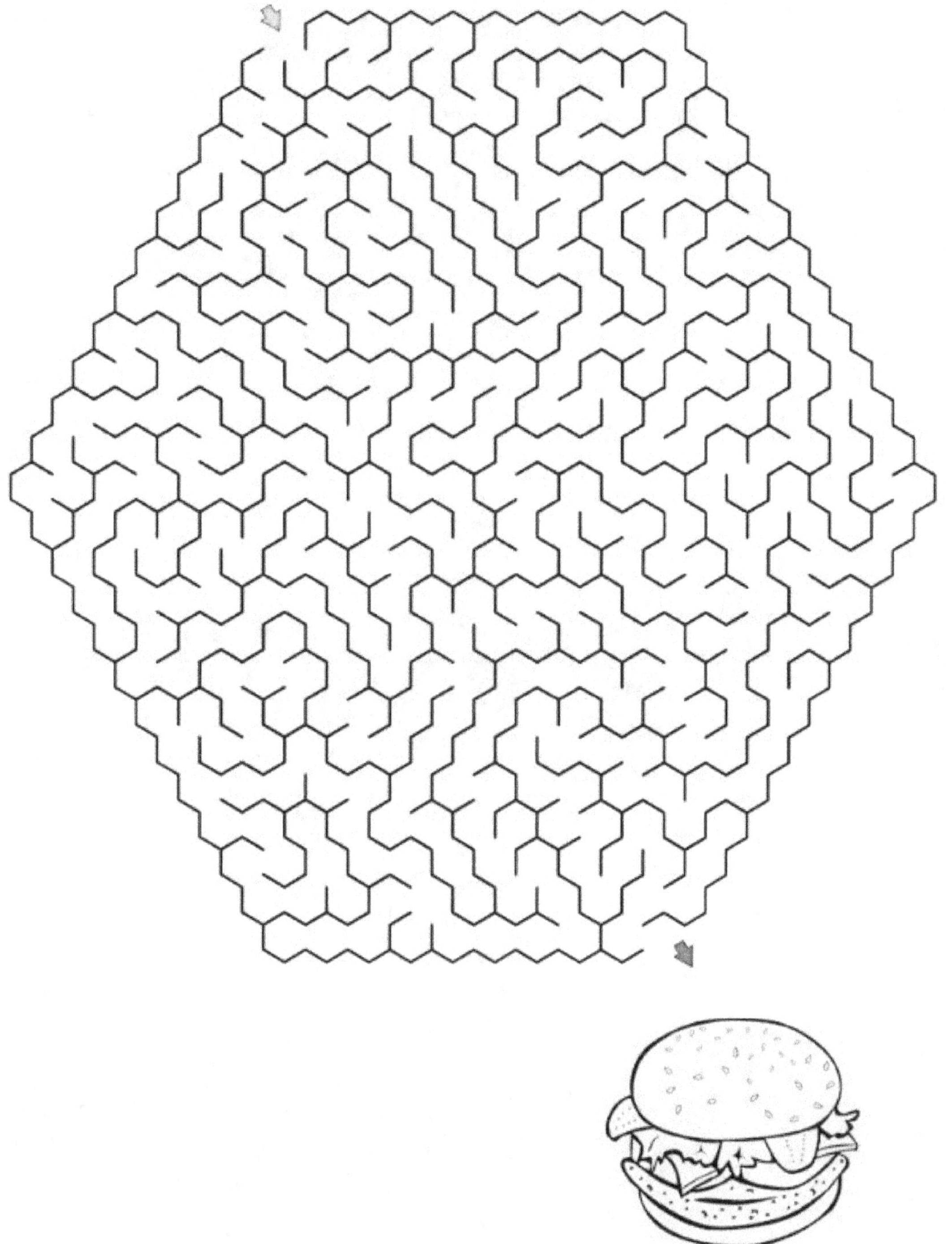

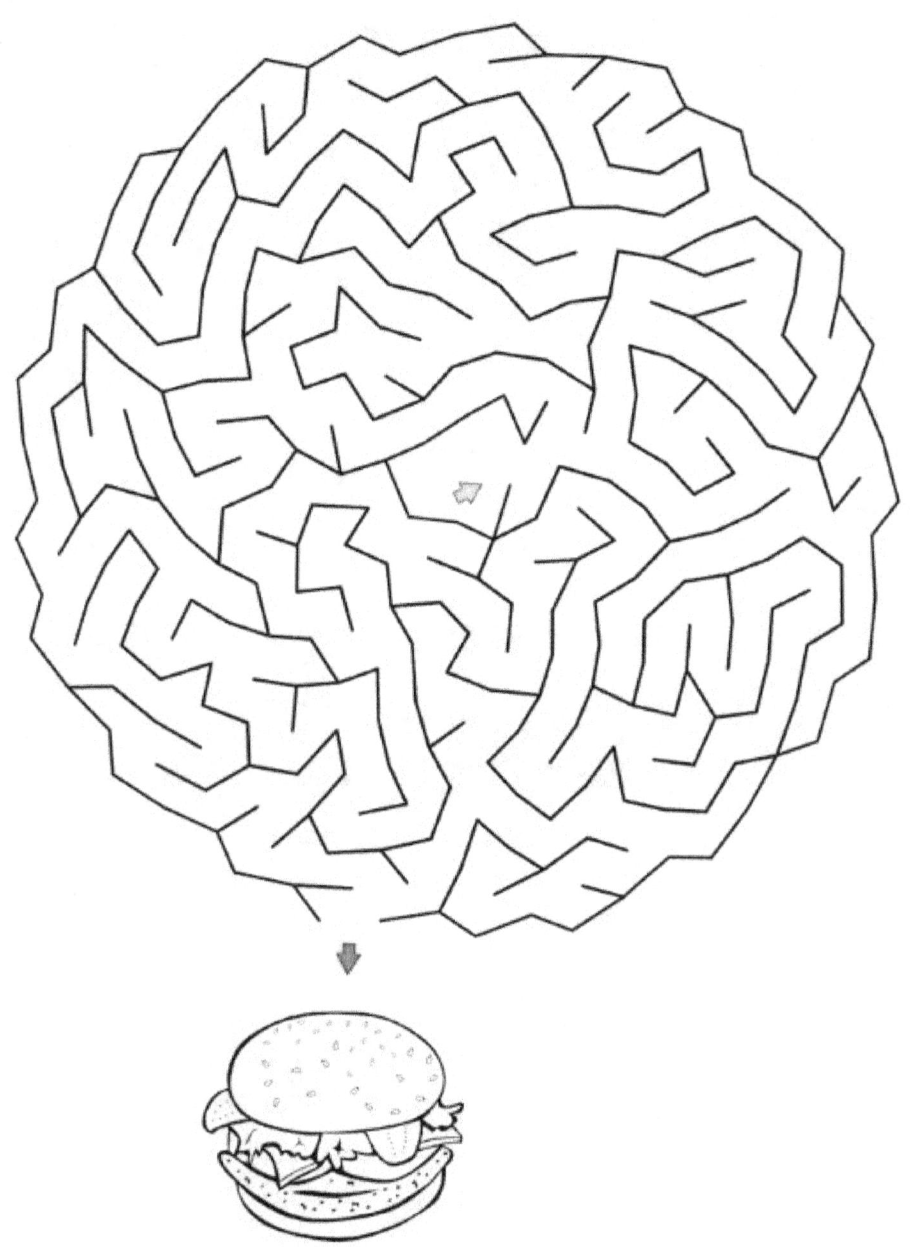

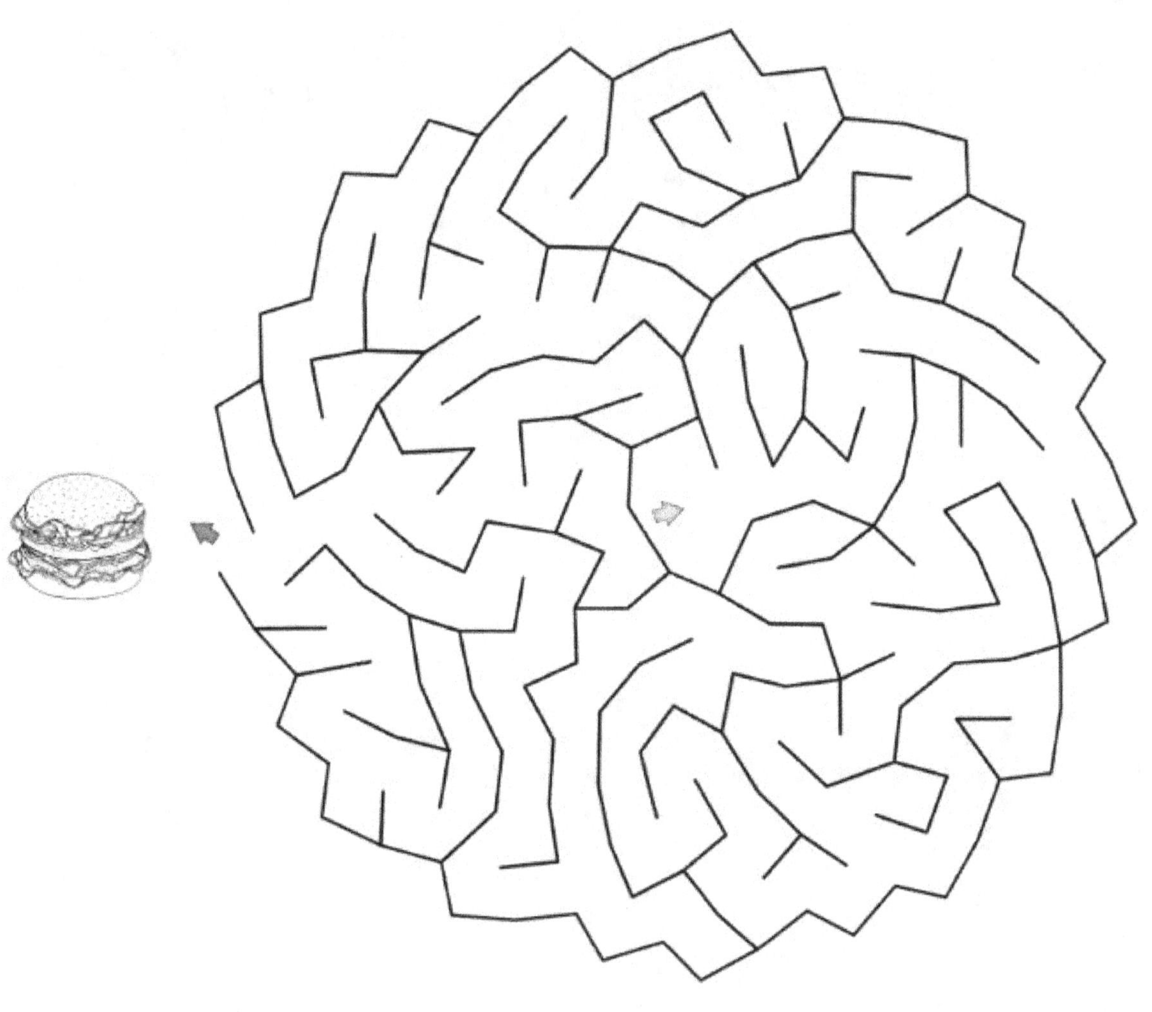

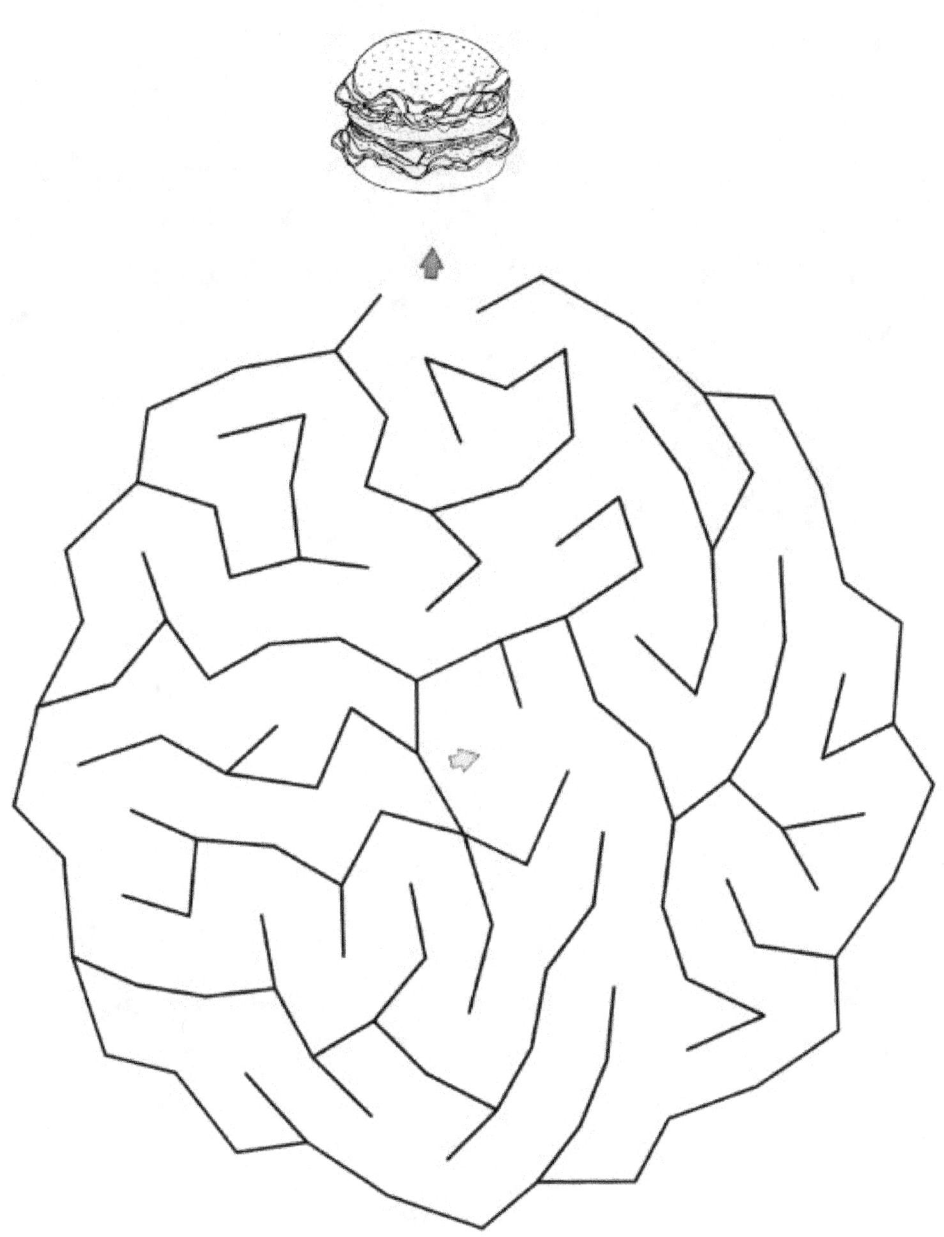

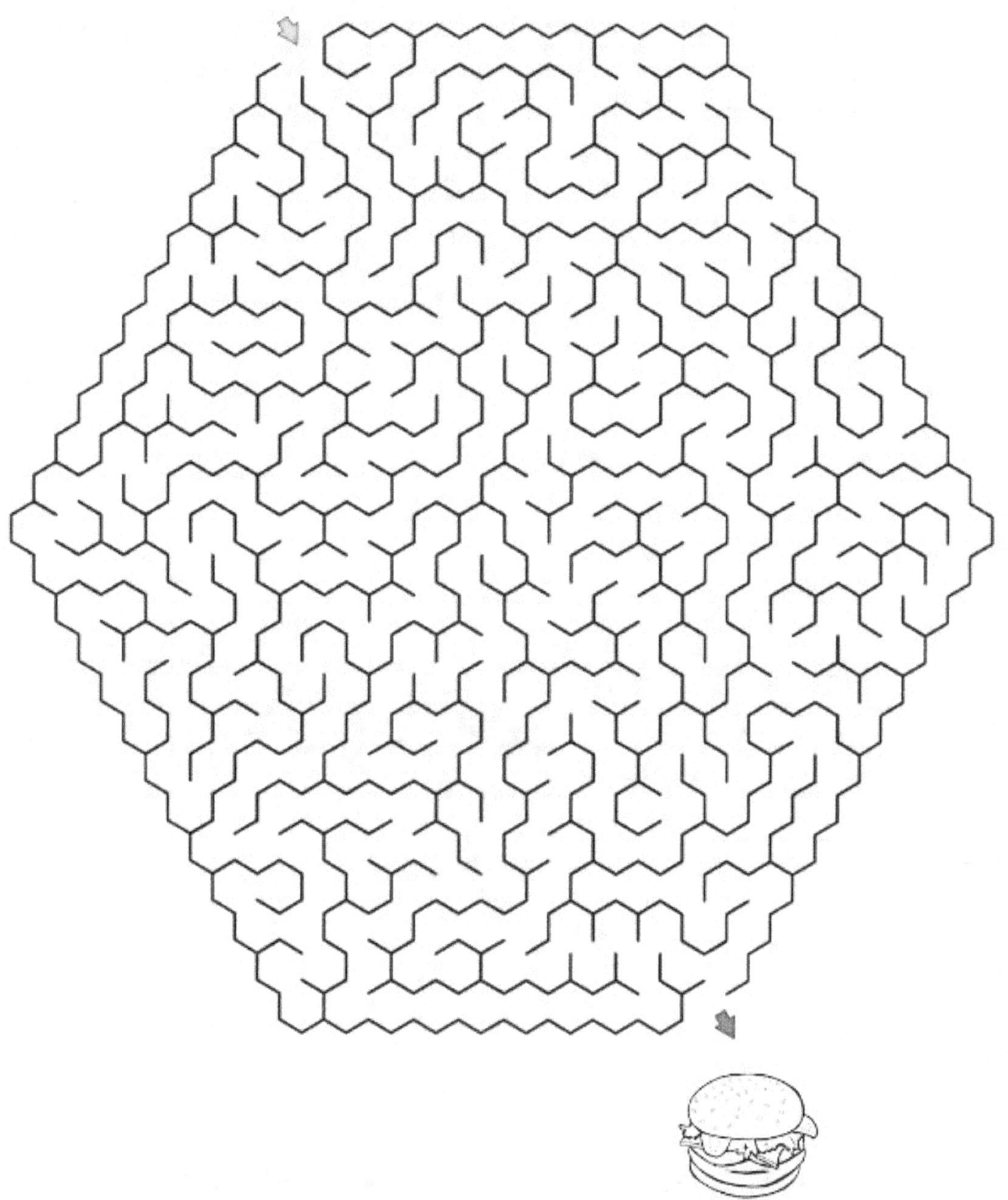

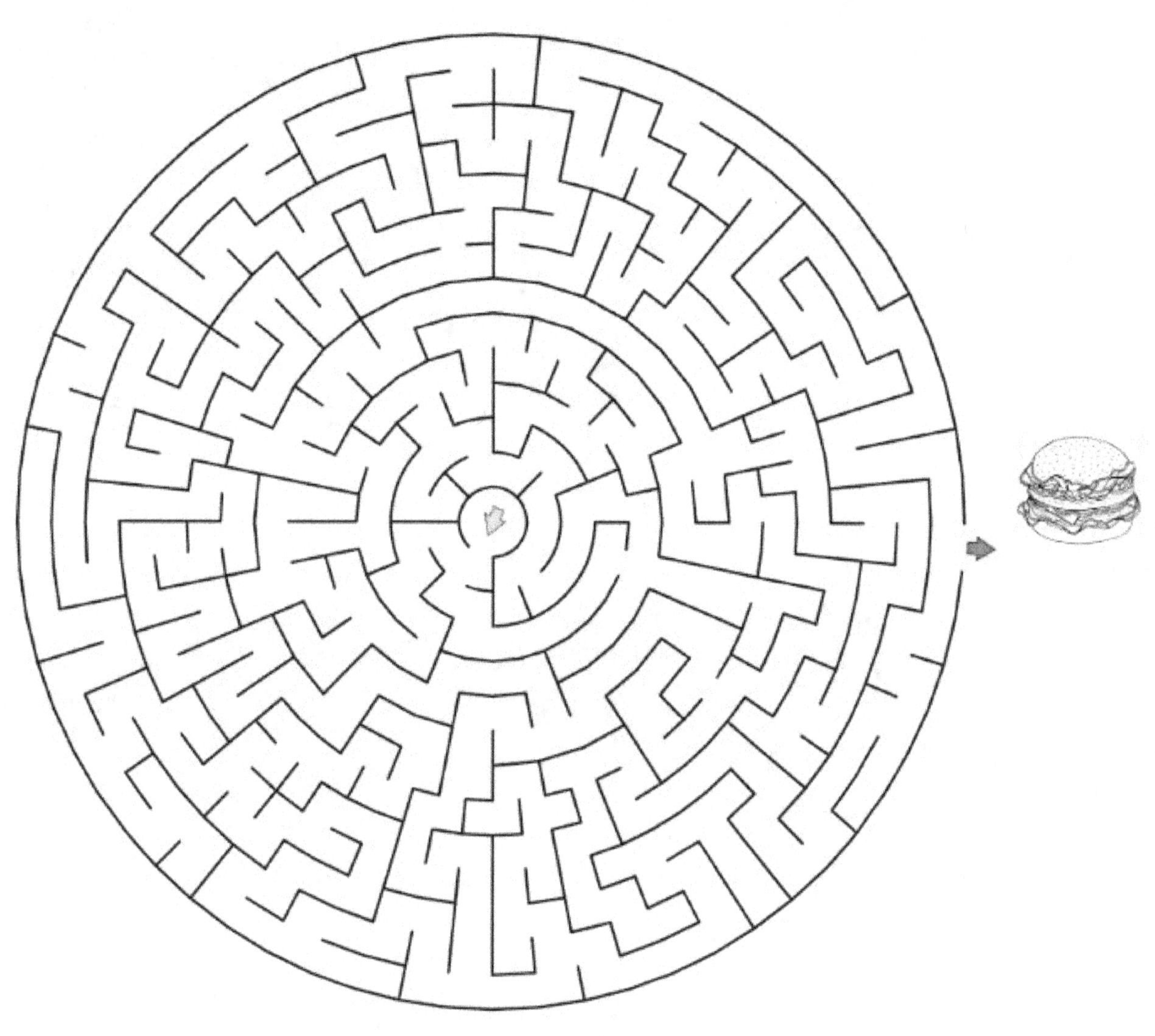

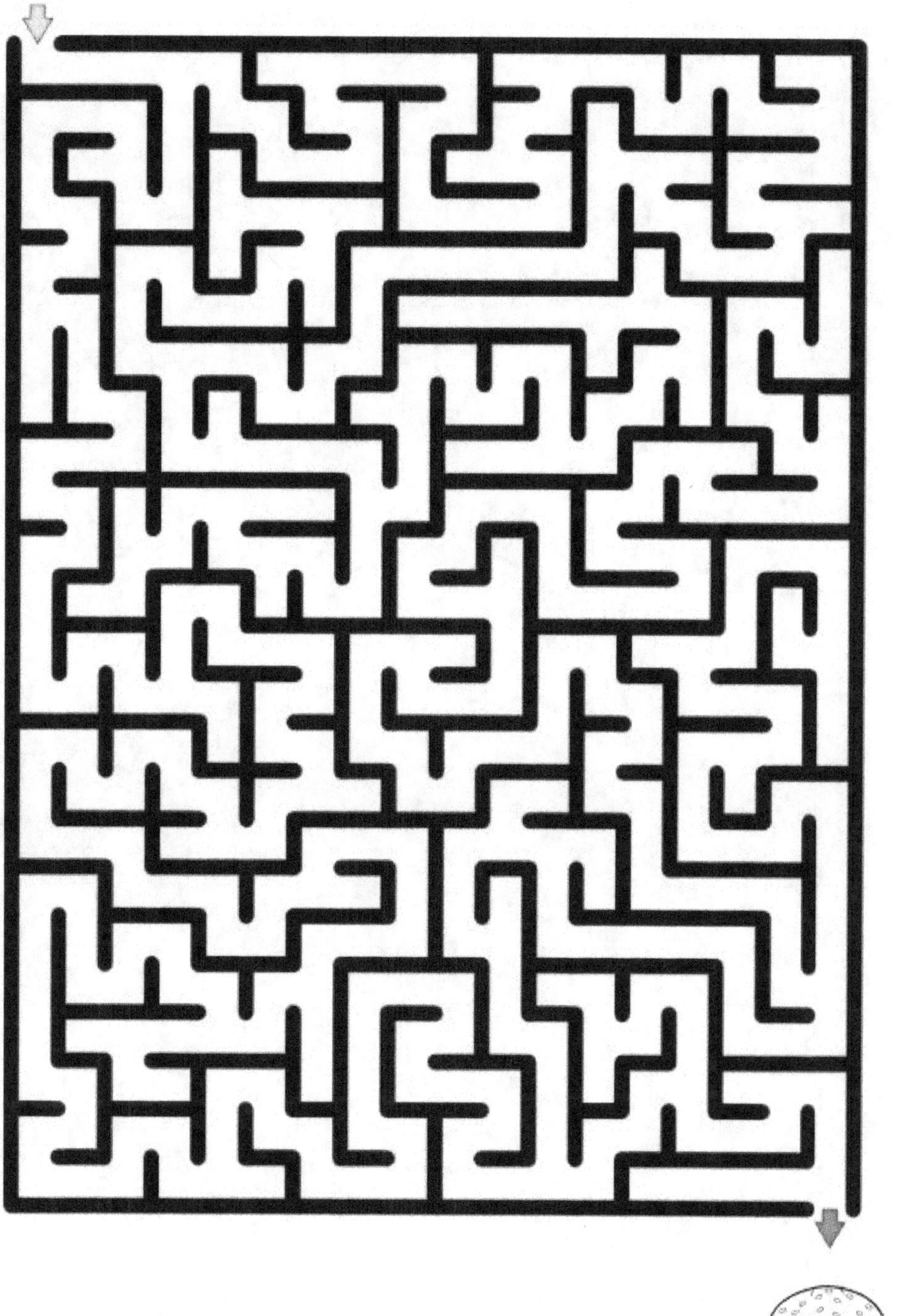

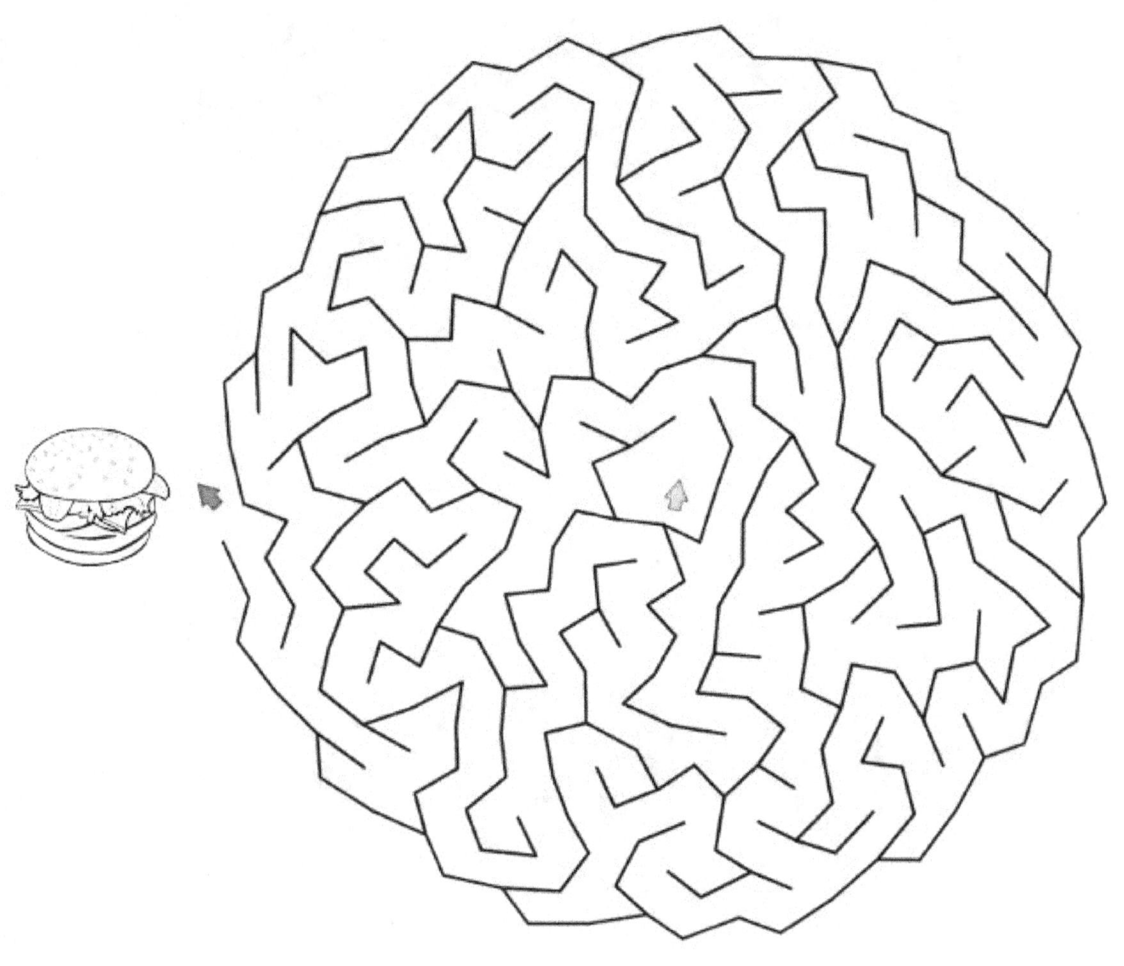

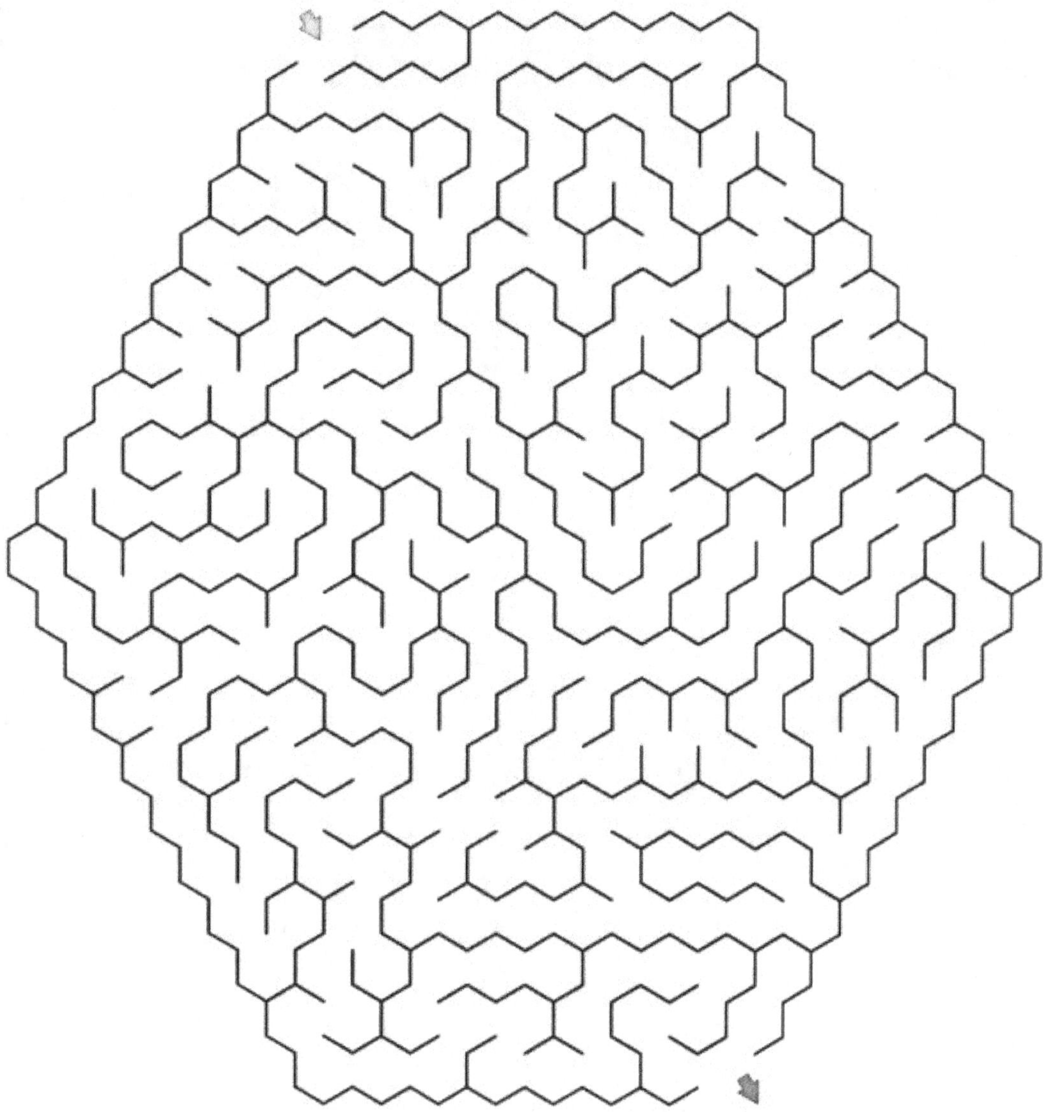

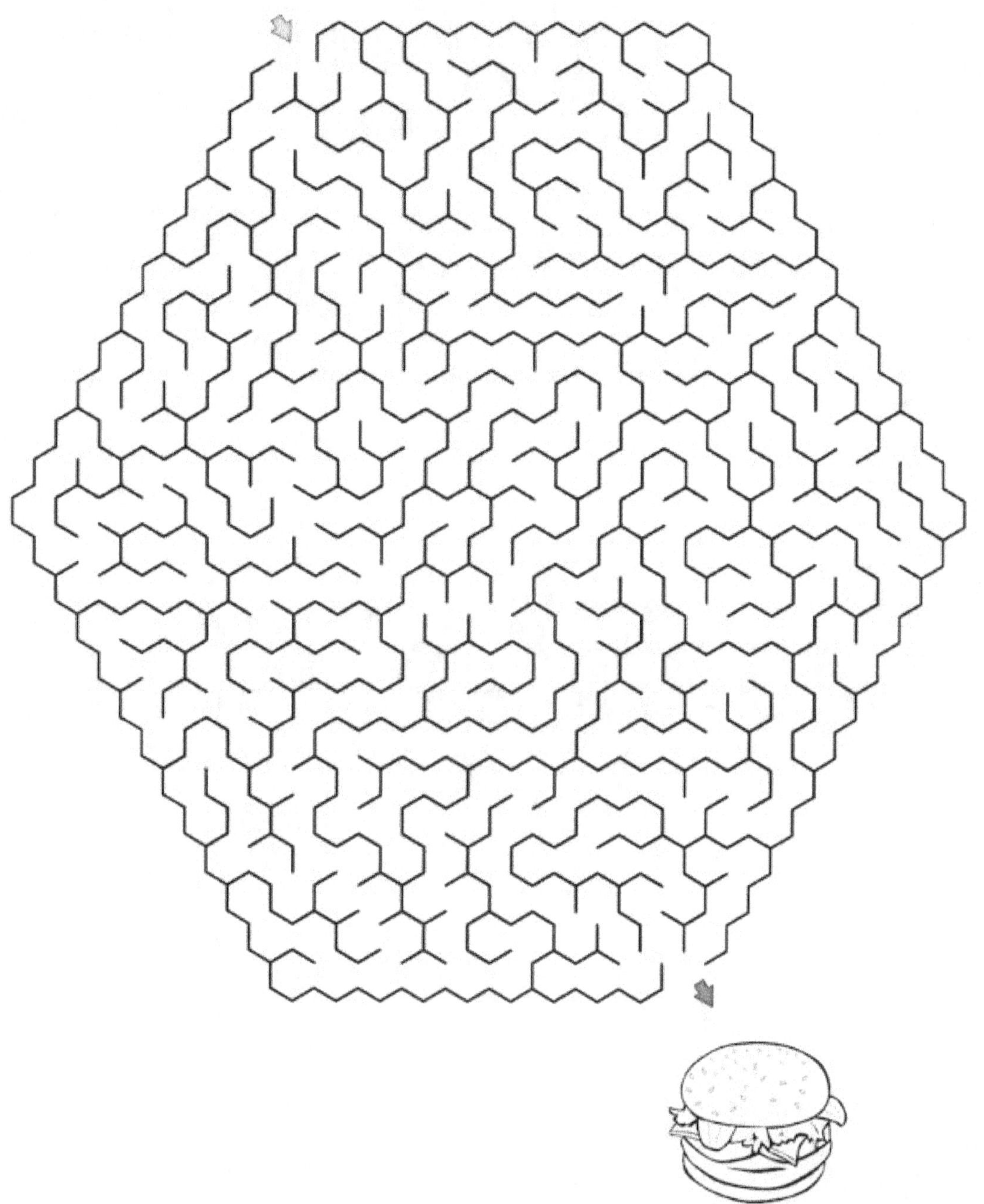

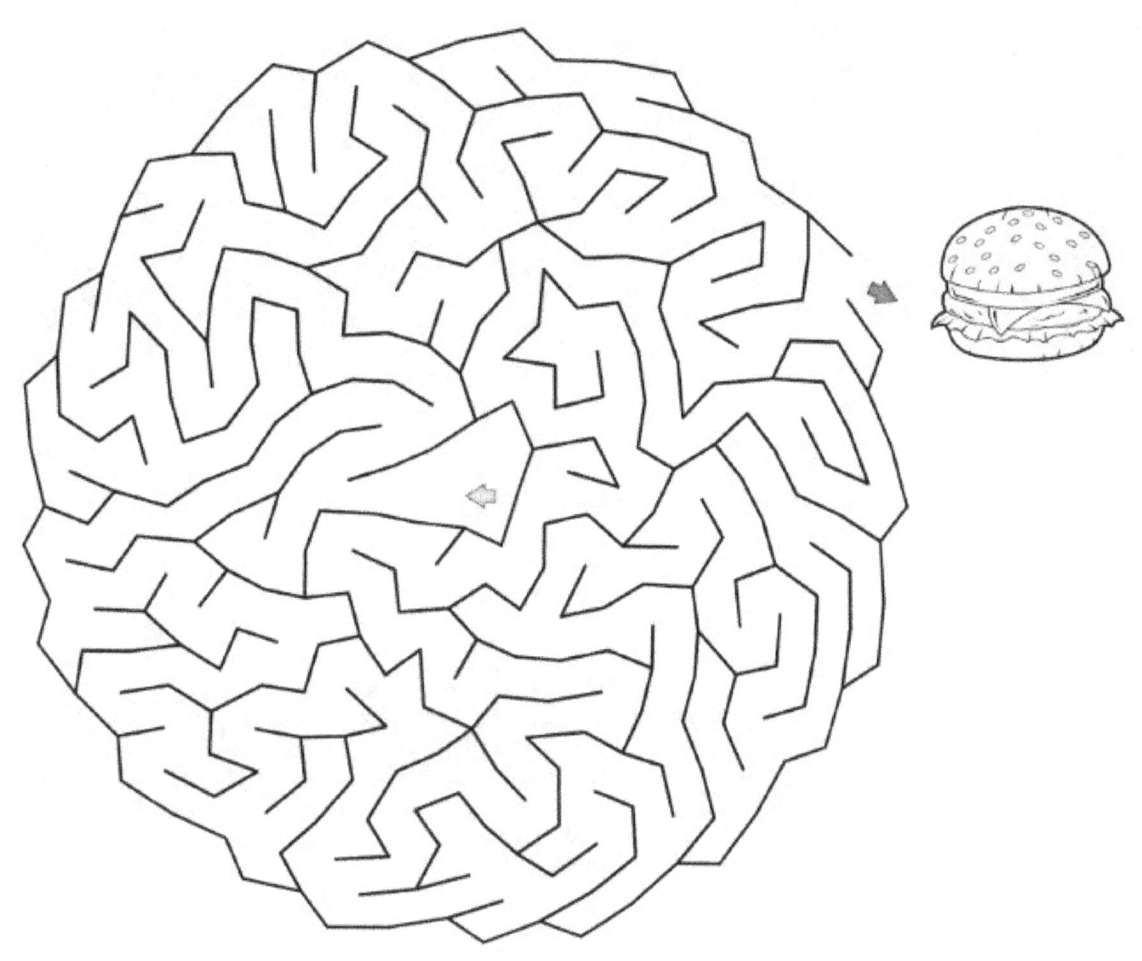

www.ingramcontent.com/pod-product-compliance
Lightning Source LLC
Chambersburg PA
CBHW081738250726
48657CB00010B/3320